DEAR *you*

HaPPY BiRTH DaY!

BY
Robie Rogge

U

UNION
SQUARE
& CO.

NEW YORK

YOUR BIRTHDAY: _____

On this day, you deserve more than
a Happy Birthday card.

With abundant good wishes,

TO: _____

FROM: _____

*Your birthday, as my own,
to me is dear. . . .* **But yours
gives most:** *for mine did only
lend me to the world;*
**yours gave to me
a friend.**

Martial, March I, 40 AD

HAPPY BI

I looked for the perfect birthday card for you—something with a message that would speak to you personally and also show my appreciation and understanding of what makes you unique.

Instead of that one card with the right message, however, I chose this collection that gives you a lifetime of wishes: more than 100 quotes of celebration, wisdom, and joy. From reckless youth to steady middle age, to the advantages and comforts of old age, this book will carry you forward year by year with a smile. And because this is a celebration of birthdays, it also includes the birthdates of the contributors, from the earliest, Roman poet Martial, March 1, 40 AD, to the most recent, Canadian actor William Vaughan, September 26, 1984.

You might have fun seeing whether any of the contributors—writers, actors, musicians, statesmen, artists, and others—shares your birthday. In this collection of 105 individuals quoted, there are twenty-four people who share twelve birthdays; your chances of a match are about 1 in 4.

THDay!

Any meaning you find in a match, however, is up to you. Two satirists (Jonathan Swift and Mark Twain) share the same birthday, but so do the polymath Ben Franklin and singer-actress Eartha Kitt.

The quotes have been carefully curated and paired to provide sources of insight, reflection, and entertainment on your birthday. Oscar Wilde observes that the old believe everything, the middle-aged suspect everything, and the young know everything. The quote on the opposite page by C. S. Lewis predicts that someday you will be old enough to read fairy tales again. Daniel-François-Esprit Auber laments that aging is the only way to live a long life, while Doug Larson, opposite, observes that life expectancy would grow by leaps and bounds if only green vegetables smelled as good as bacon. Interspersed among these pairs are single quotations worthy of their own space.

Many happy returns to someone who deserves at least 100 times more than a single birthday wish!

It is lovely, when I forget all birthdays, including my own, to find that **somebody remembers me.**

—

Ellen Glasgow, April 22, 1873

I find nothing so dear as that which is given me.

—

Michel de Montaigne, February 28, I533

I'm youth,
I'm joy,
I'm a
little bird
that has
broken out of
the egg.

J. M. BARRIE, May 9, 1860

To be
astonished
is one of
the surest
ways of not
growing
old too
quickly.

Colette
January 28,
1873

If you carry
your childhood
with you,
**you never
become
older.**

—

Abraham Sutzkever, July 15, 1913

Age does not diminish
the extreme disappointment of
having a scoop of ice cream
fall from the cone.

—

Jim Fiebig, October 3, 1956

THE OLD
believe everything;
THE MIDDLE-AGED
suspect everything;
THE YOUNG
know everything.

—

OSCAR WILDE
October 16, 1854

Some day you will be
old enough to

Start Reading
Fairy Tales Again.

—

C. S. Lewis
November 29, 1898

The young do not know enough to be prudent, and so they **attempt the impossible, and achieve it,** generation after generation.

—

Pearl S. Buck, June 26, 1892

Let's tell young people
THE BEST
books are yet to be
written; the best painting,
the best government, the
best of everything
IS YET TO
BE DONE
by them.

—

John Erskine, October 5, 1879

When I was **One,**
I had just begun.
When I was **Two,**
I was nearly new.
When I was **Three,**
I was hardly me.
When I was **Four,**
I was not much more.

When I was **Five,**
I was just alive.
But now I am **Six,**
I'm as clever as clever.
So I think **I'll be six now
for ever and ever.**

A. A. Milne, January 18, 1882

There is
still no cure for
the common
birthday.

John Glenn
July 18, 1921

I'm just the same age I've always been.

—

Carolyn Wells, June 18, 1862

At sixteen I was

stupid, confused, insecure and indecisive.

At twenty-five I was

wise, self-confident, prepossessing and assertive.

At forty-five I am

stupid, confused, insecure and indecisive.

Who would have
supposed that maturity
is only a short break
in adolescence

Jules Feiffer, January 26, 1929

Maturity is
doing what you
think is best,
**even when your
mother thinks
it's a good idea.**

———

Paul Watzlawick
July 25, 1921

YOUTH is when
you are allowed
TO STAY UP LATE ON
NEW YEAR'S EVE.

MIDDLE AGE is when
you are forced to.

———

William Vaughan
September 26, 1984

Middle age is when
you are sitting home on
a Saturday night and
the phone rings and you
hope it isn't for you.

—

Ogden Nash, August 19, 1902

IT IS NEVER TOO LATE

to be what you might have been.

———

Attributed to **George Eliot,**
November 22, 1818

You're never too old TO BECOME YOUNGER.

—

Mae West, August 17, 1893

I'm sorry you are wise,
I'm sorry you are taller;
I liked you better foolish
And I liked you better smaller.

Aline Murray Kilmer, August I, 1888

A friend is
one who knows
all about you and
*loves you just
the same.*

Elbert Hubbard, June 19, 1856

Youth,
large, lusty,
loving—
youth, full of
grace, force,
fascination,

Do you know that Old Age may come after you with equal grace, force, and fascination?

Walt Whitman, May 31, 1819

*As long as one
can admire and love,*
***then one is
young forever.***

—

PABLO CASALS
December 29, 1876

Age does not protect you from love but **LOVE**, to some extent, **PROTECTS YOU FROM AGE.**

—

Jeanne Moreau
January 23, 1928

ANOTHER BELIEF OF MINE:

that everyone else my age is an adult, whereas I am merely in disguise.

—

Margaret Atwood, November 18, 1939

It is not
HOW OLD
you are,
but HOW
you are old.

Jules Renard, February 22, 1864

*We turn
not older
with years,
but newer
every day.*

—

Emily Dickinson
December 10, 1830

Yours is
that year
that counts
no season;
I can never
be sure what
age you are.

Vita Sackville-West
March 9, 1892

Our birthdays
are feathers
in the
broad wing
of time.

Jean Paul
March 21, 1763

I think all this talk about age is foolish. Every time I'm one year older, everyone else is too.

GLORIA SWANSON, March 27, 1899

I believe in loyalty. When a woman reaches an age she likes, *she should stick with it.*

—

Eva Gabor, February 11, 1919

A diplomat is a man who always remembers a woman's birthday but never remembers her age.

—

Robert Frost, March 26, 1874

The
older
the
fiddle,

the
sweeter
the
tune.

Irish proverb

Every year on your birthday, you get a chance to start new.

—

Sammy Hagar
October 13, 1947

Be true to
your own act, and
congratulate yourself
if you have done something
strange and extravagant,
and broken the monotony
of a decorous age.

—

Ralph Waldo Emerson
May 25, 1803

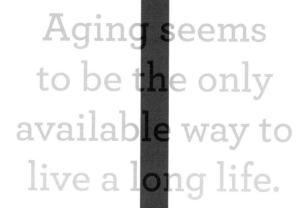

Aging seems
to be the only
available way to
live a long life.

———

Daniel-François-Esprit Auber
January 29, 1782

Life expectancy would grow by leaps and bounds if green vegetables smelled as good as bacon.

—

DOUG LARSON, February 10, 1926

Women over thirty are at their best, but men over thirty are too old to recognize it.

ATTRIBUTED TO
Jean-Paul Belmondo
April 9, 1933

The lovely thing about being forty is that you **can appreciate twenty-five-year-old men more.**

—

Colleen McCullough
June 1, 1937

THERE IS A FOUNTAIN OF YOUTH:
it is your mind, your talents,
the creativity you bring to
your life and the lives of
people you love.
*When you learn to tap into
this source, you will truly
have defeated age.*

—

SOPHIA LOREN, September 20, 1934

No age or time of life,
no position or circumstance,
has a monopoly on success.
**Any age is the right age
to start doing!**

—

RALPH W. GERARD
October 7, 1900

No one becomes forty without incredulity and a sense of outrage.

Clifford Bax, July 13, 1886

This is what 40 looks like—we've been lying for so long, who would know?

—

Gloria Steinem, March 25, 1934

One of the man
ever tells you
is that **it's such**
from being

hings **nobody**

bout middle age

nice change

oung.

DOROTHY CANFIELD FISHER, February 17, 1879

At twenty
years of age,
the will reigns;
at thirty, the wit;
and at FORTY,
the judgment.

—

BENJAMIN FRANKLIN, January 17, 1706

I am just turning **FORTY** and taking my time about it.

HAROLD LLOYD, at age 77, April 20, 1893

I have enjoyed greatly the **second blooming** *that comes when you finish the life of the emotions and of personal relations; and suddenly find—at the age of fifty, say—that a whole new life has opened before you, filled with things you can think about, study, or read about. . . . It is as if* **a fresh sap of ideas and thoughts** *was rising in you.*

———

AGATHA CHRISTIE, September 15, 1890

We in middle age require adventure.

Carolyn Gold Heilbrun
(pen name: Amanda Cross)
January 13, 1926

Life would be infinitely happier if we could only be born at the age of eighty and gradually approach eighteen.

MARK TWAIN, November 30, 1835

She said she was approaching forty and I couldn't help but wonder from what direction.

BOB HOPE, May 29, 1903

Middle age is
when you're
faced with two
temptations, and
you choose
the one that will
get you home by
nine o'clock.

—

RONALD REAGAN, February 6, 1911

The first sign of maturity is the discovery that the volume control also turns to the left.

—

JERRY M. WRIGHT
December 7, 1965

¿

How old would you be if you didn't know how old you was?

—

LEROY "SATCHEL" PAIGE, July 7, 1906

?

To me, old age is always **FIFTEEN YEARS OLDER THAN I AM.**

—

BERNARD BARUCH, August 19, 1870

Middle age is that perplexing time of life when we hear two voices calling us.

One saying,
"WHY NOT?"

And the other,
"WHY BOTHER?"

SYDNEY J. HARRIS, September 14, 1917

LIVE AS IF
you were to die
tomorrow.
LEARN AS IF
you were to live
forever.

ATTRIBUTED TO

Mahatma Gandhi, October 2, 1869

I am learning
all the time.
**The tombstone will
be my diploma.**

—

EARTHA KITT, January 17, 1927

MIDDLE AGE is
the time when a man
is always thinking
that in a week
or two he will feel
as good as ever.

—

Don Marquis, July 29, 1878

MIDDLE AGE is
when your
classmates are
so gray and
wrinkled and bald
they don't
recognize you.

—

BENNETT CERF
May 25, 1898

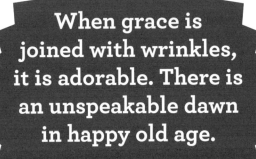

When grace is joined with wrinkles, it is adorable. There is an unspeakable dawn in happy old age.

—

VICTOR HUGO
February 26, 1802

Wrinkles should merely indicate where smiles have been.

MARK TWAIN
November 30, 1835

Middle age is
when your

BROAD MIND

 and

NARROW WAIST

begin to
change places.

As you get older,
the pickings get slimmer,
but the people don't.

—

Carrie Fisher, October 21, 1956

There are three stages of man:
he believes in **SANTA CLAUS,**
he does not believe
in SANTA CLAUS,
HE IS SANTA CLAUS.

—

BOB PHILLIPS, June 23, 1951

**THERE ARE
THREE AGES
OF MAN:**

YOUTH,

MIDDLE AGE,

and

**"GEE, YOU
LOOK GOOD."**

—

RED SKELTON
July 18, 1913

AGE is something that **doesn't** **MATTER**

Unless you're a **CHEESE.**

Billie Burke, August 7, 1884

You can only
be young once.
But you can always
be immature.

—

DAVE BARRY, July 3, 1947

AGE is a **VERY HIGH PRICE** to pay for **MATURITY.**

—

TOM STOPPARD
July 3, 1937

No man is ever old enough to know better.

—

HOLBROOK JACKSON
December 31, 1874

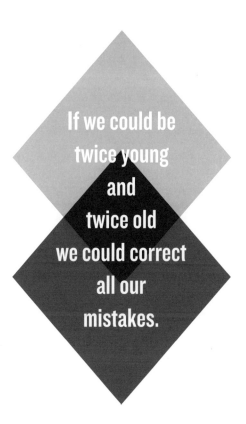

If we could be twice young
and
twice old
we could correct
all our
mistakes.

EURIPIDES, c. 484 BC

We do not grow absolutely, chronologically. We grow sometimes in one dimension, and not in another; unevenly. We grow partially. We are relative. We are mature in one realm, childish in another. The past, present, and future mingle and pull us backward, forward, or fix us in the present.

Anaïs Nin, February 21, 1903

There are years that ask questions and years that answer.

—

ZORA NEALE HURSTON
January 7, 1891

SUCCESS

is like reaching an important birthday
and finding you're exactly the same.

—

AUDREY HEPBURN, May 4, 1929

Today you are You,
that is truer than true!
There is no one alive
who is Youer than you!

—
Dr. Seuss
March 2, 1904

Inside every
old person is
a **young person**
wondering what
happened.

———

Terry Pratchett
April 28, 1948

It takes
a very
long
time

to become young.

PABLO PICASSO
October 25, 1881

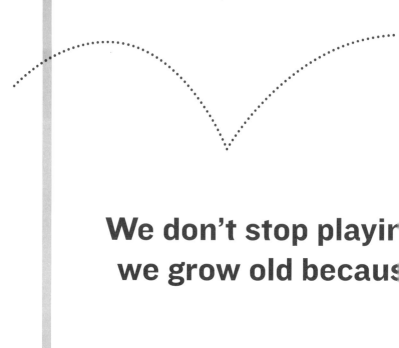

We don't stop playir
we grow old becaus

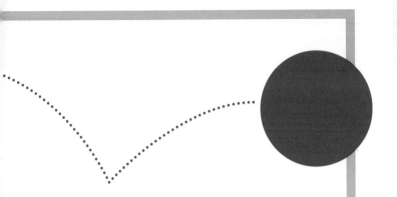

ecause we grow old,
e stop playing.

EORGE BERNARD SHAW, July 26, 1856

"OH! Well, many happy returns of the day, Eeyore."

"And many happy returns to you, Pooh Bear."

"But it isn't my birthday."

"No, it's mine."

"But you said 'Many happy returns'—"

"Well, why not? You don't always want to be miserable on my birthday, do you?"

———

A. A. MILNE, January 18, 1882

**They gave it me—for
an un-birthday present.**

———

Lewis Carroll, January 27, 1832

The young
FEEL TIRED
at the end of an
action—the old at
the beginning.

—

T. S. Eliot
September 26, 1888

I am pushing sixty years of age ... and that's enough exercise for me.

—

Mark Twain
November 30, 1835

One of the delights known to age, and beyond the grasp of youth, is that of **NOT GOING.**

———

J. B. Priestley
September 13, 1894

I have reached
an age where
if somebody tells me
to wear socks,

I DON'T HAVE TO.

Albert Einstein
March 14, 1879

Growing old is compulsory

—

growing up is optional.

Bob Monkhouse, *June 1, 1928*

I have always
believed in
the adage that
**THE SECRET TO
ETERNAL YOUTH**
is arrested
development.

—

Alice Roosevelt Longworth
February 12, 1884

To be **SEVENTY YEARS YOUNG** is sometimes far more cheerful and hopeful than to be **FORTY YEARS OLD.**

—

OLIVER WENDELL HOLMES SR.
August 29, 1809

I woke up this morning
and *I was still alive,*
so I am pretty cheerful.

—

SPIKE MILLIGAN, age 79
April 16, 1918

The SECRET OF STAYING YOUNG is to

LIVE HONESTLY,

EAT SLOWLY,

and

LIE ABOUT YOUR AGE.

LUCILLE BALL, August 6, 1911

Grow old along with me!
The best is yet to be,
*The last of life, for which the
first was made.*

—

ROBERT BROWNING, May 7, 1812

To me, fair friend, you never can be old.

—

WILLIAM SHAKESPEARE
April 23, 1564

OLD AGE has
its pleasures, which,
though different,
are not less than
the pleasures of **YOUTH.**

—

SOMERSET MAUGHAM
January 25, 1874

No wise man
ever wished
to be younger.

Jonathan Swift
November 30, 1667

Do not worry about
**AVOIDING
TEMPTATION.**
As you grow older,
**IT WILL
AVOID YOU.**

Joey Adams, January 6, 1911

They tell you that **you will lose your mind** when you grow older; What they don't tell you is that **you won't miss it very much.**

—

MALCOLM CROWLEY
August 24, 1898

Birthdays are GOOD FOR YOU; the more you have, THE LONGER YOU LIVE.

—

ANONYMOUS

I intend to live forever. So far, so good.

—

STEVEN WRIGHT
December 6, 1955

In youth

WE LEARN;

in age

WE UNDERSTAND.

———

Marie von Ebner-Eschenbach
September 13, 1830

The fact was I didn't want to look my age, but I didn't want to act the age I wanted to look either. I also wanted to grow old enough to understand that sentence.

—

Erma Bombeck, February 21, 1927

LET EVERY BIRTHDAY BE A FESTIVAL,

a time when the gladness of the house finds expression in flowers, in gifts, in a little fête. Never should a birthday be passed over without note, or as if it were a common day, never should it cease to be a garlanded milestone in the road of life.

MARGARET ELIZABETH SANGSTER
February 22, 1838

My idea of

HELL

is to be

YOUNG AGAIN.

MARGE PIERCY, March 31, 1936

Aging is
not lost youth
but a new stage of
opportunity and
strength.

—

Betty Friedan, February 4, 1921

I believe the second half
of one's life is meant to be
better than the first half.

———

**The first half is finding
out how you do it. And the
second half is enjoying it.**

FRANCES LEAR, July 14, 1923

For the unlearned, old age is winter; for the learned, it is the season of the harvest.

— **TALMUD**

Old age is an excellent time for outrage. My goal is to **say or do at least one outrageous thing every week.**

—

Maggie Kuhn
August 3, 1905

THE GREAT THING about getting older is that you become more mellow. Things aren't as black and white, and you become much more tolerant. You can see the good in things much more easily rather than getting enraged as you used to do when you were young.

—

MAEVE BINCHY, May 28, 1939

Well, I'll tell you, young fella, to be
truthful and honest and frank about it,

I'M EIGHTY-THREE YEARS OLD,
WHICH AIN'T BAD.

To be truthful and honest and frank
about it, the thing I'd like to be
right now is an astronaut.

Casey Stengel
July 30, 1890

I HOPE I NEVER RECOVER FROM THIS

[a trip to space at the age of 90].

William Shatner
March 22, 1931

YOU CAN LIVE TO BE A HUNDRED *if you give up all the things that make you want to live to a hundred.*

—

Woody Allen, December 1, 1935

X X X X X

**LIFE'S A TOUGH
PROPOSITION, and
the first hundred
years are the
hardest.**

—

Wilson Mizner, May 19, 1876

X X X X X

"In my youth," Father
William replied to
his son,

"I feared it might
injure the brain;

"But now that I'm
perfectly sure
I have none,

"Why, I do it again
and again."

"You are old, Father
William," the young
man said,

"And your hair has
become very white;

"And yet you
incessantly stand on
your head—

"Do you think at your
age, it is right?"

The first fact about the celebration of birthdays is that it is a way of AFFIRMING defiantly, and even flamboyantly, that IT IS A GOOD THING TO BE ALIVE.

———

G. K. CHESTERTON, May 29, 1874

For years
I wanted to
be older, and
*now **I am.***

———

Margaret Atwood
November 18, 1939

UNION SQUARE & CO. and the distinctive
Union Square & Co. logo are trademarks of
Sterling Publishing Co., Inc.

UNION SQUARE & CO.

NEW YORK

Union Square & Co., LLC, is a subsidiary of
Sterling Publishing Co., Inc.

Text compilation © 2023 ROBIE LLC

Illustrations © 2023 Union Square & Co., LLC

ISBN 978-1-4549-4851-3

For information about custom editions, special
sales, and premium purchases, please contact
specialsales@unionsquareandco.com.

Printed in China

2 4 6 8 10 9 7 5 3 1

unionsquareandco.com

Cover and Interior Design by Joe Newton & Maria Clavijo

HAPPY BIRTHDAY
WELL WISHES
HAPPY BIRTHDAY TO YOU!
PARTY!
JOY! JOY! JOY!
LOVE
HAPPY BIRTHDAY!
BIRTHDAY TO YOU HAPPY
IT'S YOUR SPECIAL DAY
LUV! LUV!! LUV!!! LUV!!!!
WELL WISHES
HAPPY BIRTHDAY 2
MAY YOUR WISHES COME TRUE
CELEBRATING YOU
HBD FRIEND!
HAPPY
LOVE
BIRTHDAY!
BEST WISHES
HAPPY HAPPY HAPPY
HAPPY HAPPY HAPPY
BIRTHDAY
CELEBRATION